THE NORTON LIBRARY

Medea

SHEILA MURNAGHAN is the Alfred Reginald Allen Memorial Professor of Greek at the University of Pennsylvania. She is the author of *Disguise and Recognition in the Odyssey* and numerous articles on Greek epic and tragedy, gender in classical culture, and classical reception. She is the co-author of *Childhood and the Classics: Britain and America, 1850–1965* and co-editor of *Hip Sublime: Beat Poets and the Classical Tradition, Odyssean Identities in Modern Cultures: The Journey Home*, and *Women and Slaves in Classical Culture: Differential Equations*.

THE NORTON LIBRARY

2021–2022

Euripides, Medea
  Translated by Sheila Murnaghan

Sophocles, Oedipus Tyrannos
  Translated by Emily Wilson

Aristophanes, Lysistrata
  Translated by Aaron Poochigian

Murasaki, The Tale of Genji
  Translated and Abridged by Dennis Washburn

Locke, Second Treatise of Government
  Edited by A. John Simmons

Rousseau, Discourse on the Origin of Inequality
  Translated by Julia Conaway Bondanella and Edited by Frederick Neuhouser

Shelley, Frankenstein
  Edited by Michael Bérubé

Mill, Utilitarianism
  Edited by Katarzyna de Lazari-Radek and Peter Singer

Dostoevsky, Notes from Underground
  Translated by Michael R. Katz

Woolf, Mrs. Dalloway
  Edited by Merve Emre

For a complete list of titles in the Norton Library, visit
wwnorton.com/norton-library

THE NORTON LIBRARY

Euripides
Medea

Translated by

Sheila Murnaghan

W. W. NORTON & COMPANY
Independent Publishers Since 1923

W. W. Norton & Company has been independent since its founding in 1923, when William Warder Norton and Mary D. Herter Norton first published lectures delivered at the People's Institute, the adult education division of New York City's Cooper Union. The firm soon expanded its program beyond the Institute, publishing books by celebrated academics from America and abroad. By midcentury, the two major pillars of Norton's publishing program—trade books and college texts—were firmly established. In the 1950s, the Norton family transferred control of the company to its employees, and today—with a staff of five hundred and hundreds of trade, college, and professional titles published each year—W. W. Norton & Company stands as the largest and oldest publishing house owned wholly by its employees.

Editor: Pete Simon
Associate Editor: Katie Pak
Project Editor: Maura Gaughan
Manufacturing by LSC Communications
Compositor: Westchester Publishing Services
Book design by Marisa Nakasone
Production manager: Jeremy Burton

Library of Congress Cataloging-in-Publication Data

Names: Euripides, author. | Murnaghan, Sheila, 1951– translator.
Title: Medea / Euripides ; translated by Sheila Murnaghan.
Other titles: Medea. English (Murnaghan) | Norton library.
Description: New York, N.Y. : W. W. Norton & Company, 2021. |
    Series: The Norton library | Includes bibliographical references.
Identifiers: LCCN 2020056240 | ISBN 9780393870848 (paperback) |
    ISBN 9780393885309 (epub)
Subjects: LCSH: Medea, consort of Aegeus, King of Athens (Mythological
    character)—Drama. | Revenge—Drama. | Infanticide—Drama. |
    LCGFT: Drama. | Tragedies (Drama)
Classification: LCC PA3975.M4 M77 2021 | DDC 882/.01—dc23
LC record available at https://lccn.loc.gov/2020056240

ISBN: 978-0-393-87084-8 (pbk.)

W. W. Norton & Company, Inc., 500 Fifth Avenue, New York, N.Y. 10110
www.wwnorton.com

W. W. Norton & Company Ltd., 15 Carlisle Street, London W1D 3BS

1 2 3 4 5 6 7 8 9 0

Contents

Introduction

How can a mother willingly kill her own children? That question haunts Euripides' *Medea* and has shaped hundreds of retellings of the Medea story since the play was first produced at the Festival of Dionysus in Athens in 431 B.C.E. Like all tragic playwrights of his time, Euripides was dramatizing a longstanding, well-known myth. But he was also free to reinvent its details, and his audience would have been eager to see what twist he was giving to a generally familiar course of events. It is likely (although not certain) that Medea's deliberate killing of her two sons was Euripides' innovation. The possibility that she might harm them is raised in ominously vague terms in the prologue, as Medea's Nurse sets the scene for this new version of the story: Medea, in a state of wounded outrage at being abandoned by her husband Jason, is unmoved by her children: "She hates her sons, gets no joy from seeing them. / I am afraid she's planning something" (lines 36–37). As the plot unfolds and Medea's plans take shape, that "something" turns out to be a course of revenge that destroys Jason's new wife, the bride's father (the king of Corinth, where the family is living), and finally the children.

Medea carries out an act that people routinely reject as inhuman and incomprehensible—beginning with her stunned victim

Jason, who sees Medea revealed as an animal or a monster—even though mothers have often purposefully killed their children under various circumstances throughout recorded history. By dramatizing the sequence of events that leads up to Medea's infanticide, Euripides shows how such a supposedly unthinkable thing can happen and challenges his audience to recognize its roots in familiar features of their own world. He provides a thrilling, terrifying portrait of a woman of exceptional powers and unyielding vengefulness, but her interactions throughout the play make it clear how normal she can appear and how much she has in common with ordinary women; she acts in response to circumstances of which she is herself a victim and that stem from the routine arrangements of classical Greek society and from unremarkable acts of blindness and selfishness on the part of others.

Medea is typical of many classical Athenian tragedies in that it focuses on shocking and transgressive events, especially violence between people bound by ties of kinship, and makes them believable. But Euripides characteristically does less than the other surviving tragedians to suggest that such events, however disturbing to their human witnesses, can be understood within a broader cosmic frame. Many characters in *Medea* call on the traditional Greek gods to notice their sufferings and make sure that justice is done, but there is no discernible divine response to Medea's actions. The play leaves its audience to find its own ways to make sense of the unthinkable as they confront forms of suffering that seem to exceed reasonable expectation and are commonly labeled "tragic."

The Myth before Euripides

Medea and Jason are central characters in the Argonaut legend, already described as "well known to all" in Homer's *Odyssey*, one of our earliest Greek texts (probably dating to the 700s B.C.E. and incorporating much older material).[1] We have no complete account that is earlier than Euripides, but we can piece together the basic contours of the traditional myth and some of its more variable features from

---

1. Homer, *Odyssey* 12.70.

brief references, fragments of lost works, depictions in vase painting, and later versions.

The hero Jason is sent out by his uncle Pelias from the Greek city of Iolcus (now known as Volos) on a dangerous mission to bring back the Golden Fleece—the prized pelt of a magical winged ram—from the kingdom of Colchis (modern-day Georgia) on the far shores of the Black Sea. Pelias has usurped the power of Jason's father and is hoping to get rid of an inconvenient heir to the throne by presenting him with this challenge. Jason commissions a ship, the *Argo*, and assembles a group of companions, known as the Argonauts. Together they sail to Colchis, where they encounter King Aeëtes, son of the sun-god Helios, and his daughter Medea. Aeëtes sets an impossible task as the price of the fleece: Jason must yoke together two fire-breathing bulls, then plow a field and sow it with dragon's teeth (which produces a crop of ferocious armed warriors). But Medea falls in love with Jason (through the intervention of his divine patron Hera, wife of Zeus, and Aphrodite, the goddess of love), and she gives him a magic potion that allows him to withstand the bulls, then helps him defeat the sown men and overcome the huge serpent or dragon who guards the fleece. As Jason and Medea escape together with the fleece, her father Aeëtes pursues them, but she devises a grisly way of slowing him down: she kills her brother Apsyrtus and tosses out pieces of his body, which Aeëtes stops to gather for burial. Back in Iolcus, Medea helps Jason take an equally gruesome revenge on Pelias. She uses her magical powers to rejuvenate a ram by chopping it into pieces and boiling it in a cauldron, then convinces Pelias's daughters to try the same procedure on him. In a variant on this motif, Medea in some versions genuinely rejuvenates Jason's old father Aeson.

After Medea's time in Iolcus, her story continues in two other Greek cities. The first is Corinth, to which in some accounts she has a genealogical connection through her father, who had migrated from Greece to Colchis. There her children die: in some versions she kills them inadvertently; in others they are killed by the Corinthians, who are angry at some sort of attack on the royal family. From Corinth, Medea travels to Athens and marries King Aegeus. This makes her the stepmother of his son Theseus, who has been raised elsewhere by his mother. When Theseus arrives unannounced in

Athens, she persuades Aegeus to send him into exile or to poison him, but he is eventually recognized as his father's son and rescued from her plots.

The fullest version that predates Euripides comes in an ode by the lyric poet Pindar written in honor of Arcesilas, an aristocrat who traced his ancestry to one of the Argonauts, around forty years before Euripides' *Medea*. Pindar mixes praise for Arcesilas with a selective account of the myth, focusing on Jason and Pelias in Iolcus; on the voyage to Colchis; on Aphrodite's use of love magic to help Jason seduce Medea "so that he might take away her respect for her parents"; on Jason's success in gaining the fleece with the help of Medea's concoctions and his abduction of "Medea the future killer of Pelias";[2] and on a prophecy delivered by Medea to Arcesilas's ancestor during the journey back to Greece. A number of tragedies that are now lost focused on particular sections of the myth. Sophocles wrote three plays concerning the events in Colchis and the return voyage. In one of his first plays, *The Daughters of Pelias*, produced in 455, Euripides dramatized the murder that Pindar refers to, and both Sophocles and Euripides wrote plays with the title *Aegeus* about the last, Athenian phase of the myth.[3]

From what we can tell, then, the audience of Euripides' *Medea* would have known Medea as a foreign princess, the granddaughter of the sun-god, skilled in the use of magical herbs and potions and gifted with prophecy, motivated by love and capable of betraying her family and committing strategic murders—but probably not as the killer of her own children.

The Context of Euripides' Version

Euripides' play was presented as part of a competition among tragic playwrights at the Festival of Dionysus, a divinity associated with wine, madness, revelry, and the theater, held in Athens every

---

2. Pindar, *Pythian Odes* 4.218, 250.

3. We have some scattered, inconclusive evidence about a *Medea* by another tragedian, Neophron, a contemporary of Euripides whose works are all now lost. This was so close to Euripides' version in several details, including Medea's willful killing of the children, that some ancient scholars claimed Euripides had copied it; modern scholars generally conclude the opposite, that the play in question was influenced by Euripides.

spring. This festival was a religious and political occasion, on which the city worshipped one of the major Olympian gods while also celebrating its own achievements and showing them off to visiting foreigners. In addition to drama and other kinds of poetic performance, the festival included a procession and animal sacrifice dedicated to the god, displays of financial tribute from Athens's allies, a parade of orphaned sons of men who had died fighting for the city, and the ceremonial crowning of prominent citizens.

It was typical of the Greeks to honor their gods by staging competitions in which they showed off their athletic and artistic abilities, and tragedy was a cultural achievement of which Athens was especially proud. It was at Athens, beginning in the late sixth century B.C.E., that a type of choral poetry performed by a group of singers and dancers was gradually transformed, through the addition of individual actors, into drama. In tragedy, traditional myths were acted out instead of being narrated by the chorus, which was incorporated into the story as a group of interested bystanders. Many tragic plots centered on the most violent and disturbing episodes in those myths, such as Medea's murder of her children, and those events were generally not presented directly. But the tragedians developed resources for bringing offstage occurrences to life, including vivid and detailed reports by messengers. These messengers' speeches were just one element in a spectacular multimedia performance—including spoken dialogue, choral song and dance, lyric passages sung by individual actors, and vivid costumes and scenery—that was widely admired throughout the Greek world.

Athens in 431 had a prominent place within the network of city-states that made up the Greek world. These were politically independent communities bound together by a common language and culture and involved in complex, ever-shifting alliances. Over the preceding century, the Athenians had adopted a democratic form of government and an active role in foreign affairs: they took the lead in warding off the Persians, possessors of a large and expanding empire to the east, who had invaded Greece in 490 and again in 480. In the years that followed, Athens continued to grow as a naval and sea-trading power, especially under the leadership of Pericles, a charismatic, aristocratic politician. The league formed to fight the Persians was gradually transformed into a power base that was itself a kind of empire. The city was famous for its intellectual and artistic achievements, including tragedy, comedy, and other forms of poetry, and had recently, in 438, dedicated a magnificent new temple, the Parthenon, to its patron goddess Athena. But Athens's rapidly growing power and autocratic treatment of its allies created tensions, especially with such major cities as Corinth, Thebes, and Sparta. Only a few weeks after the first performance of *Medea*, the Peloponnesian War broke out between Athens and its allies and Sparta and its allies. The war continued off and on for several decades, leaving the city drained and demoralized and finally ending with the defeat of Athens in 404—a major blow, but not the end of Athens's role as an important political and intellectual center.

The Mythic and the Ordinary

Tragedy was very much the product of fifth-century Athens, but the events dramatized in the plays belong to the legendary past and occur mostly in other places, such as Troy, Thebes, or (as in *Medea*) Corinth. As a result, there is a protective gap between the abhorrent and disruptive events of tragic plots and the city that showcased its own success by dramatizing them; when Athens figures in tragic scenarios, it is usually as an enlightened haven for struggling outsiders. But this popular, culturally central genre could also be a medium for addressing contemporary issues, offering a distant mirror for the audience's own world.

Among the three major tragedians, Euripides was seen by his contemporaries as going further than Aeschylus or Sophocles in making figures from heroic legends resemble modern Athenians in their patterns of speech and their concerns. His plays reflect the intellectual currents of the late fifth century, especially the ideas of a controversial group of thinkers known as the Sophists, who raised fundamental questions about the validity of social conventions and religious traditions, and stressed the power of human reasoning and argumentation as the basis of belief. Many Sophists were teachers of the rhetorical skills that were essential to Athenian public life, in which major political decisions were made in a popular assembly and the law courts were also an important arena of personal advancement. Although he undoubtedly calls many received truths into question, Euripides cannot be easily aligned with or against the Sophists, but we see the impact of their thought—and of Athens's rhetorical culture—throughout *Medea*. It surfaces in the characters' observations about the advantages and limits of cleverness and the effects of skillful speech, and especially in the long central debate between Medea and Jason over the rights and wrongs of their marriage, in which Jason in particular makes a number of ingenious but also dubious arguments (465–575).

The situation that Medea and Jason argue about has its origins in far-flung travel and supernatural adventures. In setting the scene, Medea's Nurse begins with Jason's fateful passage through the Clashing Rocks, the perilous, otherworldly barrier that marks the entrance to the Black Sea and represents a dividing line between the Greek world and the foreign territory outside it. But she is soon describing his and Medea's return to Greece and speaking in general terms about a wife's loyalty to her husband as the best safeguard for a marriage: the conflict between husband and wife that plays out in Corinth exposes the fault lines in a familiar institution at the heart of fifth-century Athenian society. Medea has been brought to Greece from a distant Asiatic home, but the relationship between her foreign status and what she does in the course of the play is by no means straightforward, complicating rather than affirming contemporary Athenian ideas about foreigners.

Mid-fifth-century Athens was marked by tensions around questions of ethnic identity and the integration of foreigners. The war against Persia at the beginning of the century had solidified ideas of Greek identity and especially of Greek superiority to non-Greeks, who were variously portrayed as slavish, luxury-loving, treacherous, lawless, and overly passionate; as the leaders of that struggle, the Athenians saw themselves as the chief defenders of Greek values. The distinction between Athenians and others was also reinforced by a law passed in 451 that restricted the much-prized rights of citizenship to children with an Athenian mother as well as an Athenian father.

We hear echoes of contemporary attitudes in Medea's pointed observation that Jason is abandoning her because he thinks a foreign wife will become an embarrassment (591–92) and in Jason's outburst when he learns of the children's murder: "No Greek woman would ever do that" (1339). That is an understandable reaction from a devastated victim, but many aspects of Medea and Jason's story tell against the idea that she is more like a conventional foreigner than he is. It is Jason who is conspicuously guilty of treachery. As the chorus of Corinthian women points out, Medea crossed over to the Greek world "[b]ecause of an oath" (210) overseen by Themis, the goddess associated with justice and proper order—the oath being an important Greek cultural norm that Jason has violated. When Jason claims during their debate that Medea has gained the most from their relationship because she now lives in Greece, where she benefits from justice and the rule of law (534–44), those patriotic claims ring hollow.

When Medea first appears onstage, emerging from her house to make contact with the chorus, she offers an analysis of marriage in which every wife is in essence a foreigner:

> Finding herself among strange laws and customs,
> a wife needs to be clairvoyant; she hasn't
> learned at home how to deal with her mate.   (238–40)

Medea's description of marriage is colored by unhappy experience, but its features correspond to the contemporary institution that Euripides' audience would have known. Marriage in fifth-century Athens was a transaction between male-headed households, in which a woman left her father's house and entered into the house of her husband. There her life was spent mostly inside and her most important function was child-bearing. Ideally, this was a harmonious, respectful division of labor, with each spouse pursuing the couple's shared interests in a different sphere, the husband tending to business outside the house and the wife working inside under his protection. But the prime beneficiaries of classical marriages were undoubtedly the men who arranged and controlled them: the fathers who cemented their relations with other men by giving them their daughters and the husbands who gained a means of producing heirs for their families. Although Jason's situation as an outsider advancing himself through a royal marriage also evokes a distant world, his freedom to abandon Medea when expedient is in line with Athenian law, which granted men but not women the right to divorce at will.

Medea's bitter words reveal how asymmetrical this arrangement might seem to a woman: largely confined to the house, a woman has nowhere to turn if she is lonely or unhappy, while a man can go out and find other company; men's efforts in the outside world, especially as soldiers, are more highly valued than the taxing labor of childbirth.

Fictional tragic heroines become visible and speak in a public context as real classical Athenian women did not, and Medea's unusual powers and history put her in a position to articulate and act on feelings that were not usually aired but may well have been widely experienced. The conviction that her husband ought to protect her interests, which fuels Medea's anger at Jason, reflects what any wife might justly expect, a point that Euripides makes through his use of the chorus. Every new tragedy involved the playwright in a decision about what identity to assign the chorus, a collective character whose relation to the action was usually that of an observer or bystander (although not necessarily a model for the audience) and whose songs combined the particular outlook of its fictional identity with traditional communal values. In *Medea*, Euripides chose to pair his exceptional female protagonist with a group of women who also claim an unexpected voice for themselves but are clearly identified as ordinary Corinthians. Their sympathy for Medea's grievances and support for her plans to punish Jason effectively affirm the broad relevance of her complaints.

Medea's Divided Self

Medea establishes a strong connection with the Chorus, but she is not actually herself an ordinary woman. She makes her case so compellingly that it is easy to forget the darker details of her past and the wilder aspects of her personality. When she tells them that she is worse off than they are because she has "no mother, brother, or other family / to shelter me now that disaster has struck" (257–58), she elides the fact that she willingly betrayed her father when she left home with Jason, chopping her brother into pieces as she went. Her Nurse, the person who knows her best, has already mentioned her next exploit, persuading the daughters of Pelias to kill their father, and has also given some ominous hints about her nature, introducing the comparisons between Medea and wild animals or harsh natural elements like rocks and the sea that recur throughout the play. Medea's cries from behind the stage, when she has not yet assumed her public persona, reveal something of the depth and extremity of the emotions that drive her.

Medea's exceptional nature is most fully realized in her willingness to pursue revenge to a point where the Chorus can no longer follow her with sympathy or comprehension: the killing of her own children. This difference springs not from her foreignness so much as from her investment in a set of attitudes and values typically associated with Greek men: she presents a mixture of qualities that unsettle the categories of male and female as well as the categories of Greek and non-Greek. In contracting her own marriage, she has taken upon herself a prerogative that would normally belong to her father, and she treats her arrangement with Jason as if it were a pact between two men. In particular, she portrays their marriage as an agreement secured by solemn oaths of a kind found in the male spheres of public and social life; even before she appears, we hear from the Nurse that she is "shouting about their oaths" (21). In this way, she appeals to one of the most sacred customs of the Greek world: oaths were sworn by invoking the gods, who were believed to punish those who broke them, and this fortifies her in her confidence that she is acting as a righteous, divinely backed avenger. As many critics have pointed out, Medea's determination and sense of injustice also make her more like some of the male heroes encountered in the Homeric epics and other tragedies (for example, Achilles in the *Iliad* and Ajax in Sophocles' *Ajax*) than like a conventional female character. In common with those heroes, she has a robust sense of her own honor, which she will go to any lengths to protect, and is particularly enraged by the thought that her enemies might be laughing at her.

Medea may have the tenacity and self-regard of a male hero, but she carries out her revenge by drawing on the resources of a woman—and an ordinary woman, not a divinely connected sorceress or an exotic foreigner. One of these is the deadly poison that she uses on Jason's new wife. Athenian women of the classical period were regularly suspected of resorting to poison. In a speech that survives from a fourth-century court case, for example, a man accuses his stepmother of killing his father by arranging for a deadly potion to be introduced into his after-dinner wine.[4]

Medea relies heavily on her cleverness (a trait that she and others bring up repeatedly) and especially her gift for persuasion, qualities that Greek men often attributed to women and feared in them. The brilliant performances with which she draws others to her cause make her like an actor or a stage manager, and this connects her portrayal to contemporary concerns about the deceptiveness and emotional power of the theater, which was sometimes seen as a dangerously feminine medium. The opening exchange in which she convinces the Chorus to keep quiet about her plans is only the first of a series of encounters in which Medea manipulates other people for her own ends. She talks Creon into letting her stay in Corinth just long enough that she can carry out her revenge; she gets the king of Athens, Aegeus, to agree to take her in after she leaves Corinth; and she convinces Jason that she accepts his new marriage, with the result that he helps her send lethal gifts to his new wife.

Medea's most effective means of hurting Jason is rooted in the capacity to bear children, for which women were at once valued and resented in the patriarchal world of classical Greece. For Athenians, in particular, the importance of motherhood was accentuated by the citizenship law of 451, which made having an Athenian mother a necessary qualification for citizenship. Medea skillfully exploits men's dependence on women for the offspring they want and need. She overcomes Aegeus's misgivings by promising to use her skill with drugs to solve his ongoing childlessness. And she cuts off all of Jason's, hopes by killing not only his existing children but also his second wife who, as he callously points out, could give him new ones.

Even as she internalizes male values and treats her feminine qualities as useful tools, Medea remains a mother with a powerful attachment to her sons. The Chorus's ability to identify with her breaks down when they realize that she really intends to kill the boys. This is due in part to their horror at so momentous a violation of human and divine law, but also to the fact that she is taking a step that is bound to make her "impossibly wretched" (818). Yet

---

4. Antiphon 1, "On the Stepmother."

Medea's resolve to go through with the infanticide does not mean that she ever stops feeling a mother's pain at the loss she is inflicting on herself as well as Jason. This becomes clear in the remarkable extended monologue in which she wrestles with her decision; in that speech, she reveals a painfully divided self, torn between her drive for vengeance and her maternal feelings, and so between the masculine and feminine sides of her character.

Jason's instinctive response to Medea's infanticide is to call her an animal and a freak, "an inhuman wife, a lioness / more savage than Etruscan Scylla" (1342–43). But what Medea does is more disturbing than Jason's labels can express because it arises so naturally out of circumstances and feelings that may take unusual and exaggerated forms but are fundamentally familiar and human. Unlike many later retellers of her story, Euripides insists that, even if what Medea does is abhorrent, she remains entirely sane, consciously in control of her actions and recognizably the same woman who appeared at the play's opening as a justly aggrieved victim of mistreatment.

Only at the very end of the play is Medea revealed as a superhuman figure, through a stunning theatrical effect. Hearing the news of his children's death, Jason has rushed to the house and is banging on the door. This is the same door through which the audience saw Medea enter when her mind was finally made up and through which they heard the terrified cries of the trapped boys, and they would have expected that door to open and a wheeled platform to come out, bringing the bloody scene inside into view. But suddenly Medea is heard speaking from high above, at the top of the house, lifted up by a special crane to a position normally occupied by actors playing gods. She stands in a magic chariot drawn by dragons and sent by her grandfather the Sun.

As Medea looks down on Jason, belittling his efforts and reveling in her invulnerability, she exhibits the arrogance and indifference to human suffering of which the Greek gods are capable, a theme explored in many of Euripides' plays. As she and Jason spar for the last time, he is hopelessly outmatched and sadly diminished, punished in a way that is out of proportion with his shallow, thoughtless, self-seeking behavior. Gods like Zeus and Themis, who uphold justice and good order and who have been repeatedly invoked throughout the play, are absent from this ending, apparently willing to see Medea escape unpunished. This disturbing outcome is compounded by Medea's destination: in a travesty of the city's traditional role as a safe haven for powerless outcasts, Athens will take in and protect the mother who brought herself to kill her own children.

A New Song for Women?

Jason's abandonment of Medea inspires the Chorus to sing about the one-sidedness of the poetic tradition, which abounds in stories of treacherous women, but only because they are produced by men.

> Enough of ancient poets' legends
> that tell of us as breaking faith!
> The lord of song, divine Apollo,
> did not grant the lyre's sweet music
> for the speaking of our minds,
> or I could have made an answer
> to the stories spread by men.
> Time's long record speaks on both sides.   (421–31)

These women use the voice they gain as figures in a tragic plot to imagine a different kind of song, one that would tell women's side of the story. This raises the question of whether we should see Euripides' play, with its focus on an articulate woman whose life has been ruined by her husband's exercise of male privilege, as such a song. Certainly Medea's opening speech gives a memorable analysis of the disadvantages to women of patriarchal marriage. Both Creon and Jason see her through a misogynistic lens, attributing to her the stereotypical female qualities of emotional excess, sexual obsession, and deviousness. Jason's frustration at her refusal to support his plans culminates in a generalized wish that men would not have to deal with women at all:

> We should have some other way of getting children.
> Then there would be no female race,
> and mankind would be free from trouble.   (573–75)

Medea deftly exploits these attitudes to achieve her goals. She appeals to Creon and Aegeus with displays of weepy helplessness, and persuades Jason to excuse her earlier anger with a brilliantly tentative reference to female weakness:

> Women just are . . . well, not quite wicked,
> but anyway you shouldn't copy us
> and get caught up in silly quarrels.   (889–91)

But *Medea* is a play, not a manifesto, and no character can be simply identified as speaking for the author. The wrongs that Medea has suffered call forth remarkably direct statements about the power imbalance that makes them possible. But she answers them with passionate acts of vengeance that are so vicious and so deeply destructive of the innocent as well as the guilty that they overwhelm the structural unfairness of Athenian gender arrangements. In the end, the play tells a story of devastating female treachery, and Medea herself, as she summons the strength to carry out her plan, voices a darkly self-hating view of women:

> Now Medea, use everything you know;
> . . .
> You have the skill, and along with that
> a woman's nature—useless for doing good
> but just right for contriving evil.   (401, 407–09)

It is not really possible to generalize about Euripides' view of women; in antiquity his unusually intimate portraits of women's emotional lives earned him a reputation both for a kind of proto-feminism and for misogyny (partly on the grounds that he hurt women by revealing their secrets). His interest in female psychology went together with a tendency to portray women as the first point of entry for dangerous passions that could spread through a community and undermine all of its meaningful distinctions. The play clearly raises issues that its audience needed to think about, and it might be helpful to know whether women were part of that audience. But our evidence for that question, which consists largely of scattered anecdotes, is inconclusive. We can only be sure that tragedy, which was composed by men and performed by men, presented its challenging scenarios to the city's male citizens, and we can only speculate about the lessons they drew from it.

The Afterlife of Medea

Euripides' play represents an especially influential chapter in the long and varied tradition of the Medea myth, which is still evolving in the twenty-first century, with frequent productions and new adaptations. The further retellings that survive from the classical world build on Euripides' interest in the psychology of a woman under extreme pressure and struggling with conflicting impulses. The most significant treatment by a later Greek author comes in the *Argonautica* by Apollonius of Rhodes, an epic narrative of the Argonauts' journey to Colchis written in the third century B.C.E. Unlike the earlier epics of the Homeric period, the *Argonautica* focuses on romantic love as much as heroic adventure, and one of its four books is devoted to an extensive portrait of Medea as a young woman in her father's house torn between her love for Jason and her duty as a daughter.

Medea was the subject of numerous plays by Roman authors writing in Latin, most of which are now lost. One of those was by the poet Ovid (43 B.C.E.–17 C.E.), who also treated Medea in his surviving mythological epic, the *Metamorphoses*. Like Apollonius, Ovid dwells particularly on Medea's first steps on the path of evil, depicting her inner turmoil as she debates whether to cast her lot with Jason, until she finally decides to do what she knows is wrong, fully aware that she has been undone by love. A half century later Seneca (4 B.C.E.–65 C.E.) wrote a *Medea* that closely follows Euripides' plot, but gives it a more sensational treatment. Seneca fully develops those sides of Medea that Euripides plays down or balances with competing qualities. His Medea is a bloodthirsty seeker of vengeance from the outset, a more willing pursuer of evil, and a true witch.

While Seneca's version, like his other tragedies, had an important influence on revivals of Greek tragedy from the Renaissance on, most modern versions of the myth move in the opposite direction, finding some way to make Medea's child-killing more understandable and acceptable in human terms. A version by Richard

Glover performed in London in 1767 adopts a strategy that may have been present in some pre-Euripidean variants, portraying Medea as the victim of temporary madness or "phrenzy." Over the last two centuries, many writers have responded to the possibility of making Medea a clear figure for marginalized people, whether as a woman or as a foreigner. In nineteenth-century England, her famous speech on the hard lot of wives was recited at meetings of suffragists. Medea and Jason's different origins have been variously reconceived as differences of culture and race. To give only a few examples out of many, Medea has been reenvisioned as a princess from a fictional Asian country married to a French colonial administrator (Henri Lenormand, *Asie*, 1931), as a black African bride brought home to Puritan New England by her seafaring husband (Maxwell Anderson, *The Wingless Victory*, 1936), and as an Irish traveler treated as an outcast by her well-established in-laws (Marina Carr, *By the Bog of Cats*, 1998). In Pier Paolo Pasolini's 1969 film starring Maria Callas, Medea belongs to a primitive world in close harmony with nature and divinity, while Jason represents industrialized, bourgeois modern society.

This conception of Medea as an outsider is often accompanied by the idea that she kills her children for their own good, to spare them an even worse fate (an idea that emerges in Euripides, but only after Medea has herself sealed their fate by making them the agents of her attack on Jason's new wife). This was the case with Margaret Garner, a real woman who came to be known as "the modern Medea." Garner was an escaped slave in pre–Civil War America who, when apprehended by U.S. marshals, killed her daughter to prevent her from being returned to slavery; her story became the basis of Toni Morrison's 1987 novel *Beloved*. In Guy Butler's *Demea* (written in the 1960s but first performed in 1990), a black South African Medea figure kills her children to save them from apartheid.

These are a few permutations within a vast and continuing stream of modern Medeas. They testify to the ongoing effectiveness of the Medea myth for raising questions about marriage, parenthood, sexual jealousy, ethnicity, cross-cultural relations, and the status of women, and to the extraordinary stimulus to other writers offered by Euripides' play. They also return us to Euripides' own achievement in depicting a compelling heroine who remains so difficult to classify in familiar terms of foreign and native, male and female, divine and human.

The Staging of Euripides' Play

Euripides' *Medea* was first performed along with three other plays by Euripides (two other tragedies and a light-hearted, parodic satyr play) on a single day during the annual Festival of Dionysus. The venue was an open-air theater on the slopes of the Acropolis, the commanding hill at the center of Athens. The audience, which numbered around 10,000 people, most likely all men, sat on benches on the hillside, looking down at the performance space. This consisted of a flat circular area, the *orchestra* (or dance floor), where the chorus danced and sang; behind the *orchestra* there was a raised platform holding a simple building, the *skene*, which typically represented a house, like the house of Jason and Medea. The actors appeared on this platform, coming and going through a door in the *skene* or arriving at ground level by two paths on either side of that platform. Sometimes a much smaller platform, or *ekkyklema*, would be wheeled out through the door of the *skene* as a device for showing the inside of the house, especially the aftermath of some violent event which had taken place there. This is what the audience of *Medea* probably expected to see in the final scene. Instead, Medea appeared on top of the house, lifted up by a special crane, or *mechane*, that was more often used for the appearances of gods. The actors and chorus members were all men, dressed in costumes and wearing masks. Seen from a distance in this large outdoor setting, and without the ability to change their facial expressions, they had to rely on simple and stylized gestures to supplement their words.

The text that is translated here is a script of the words that were spoken, chanted, and sung at that performance. All of the play was in verse, but part of what made tragedy an especially impressive and innovative form was the way it brought together different types of performed poetry reflected in the different styles and types of line in this translation. The long speeches and dialogue were in iambic trimeter, the meter considered closest to everyday speech, and were simply spoken. Some passages, such as the entrance of the Chorus and the more urgent utterances of Medea's Nurse, were in anapestic dimeter, a meter of shorter, more regular lines, each with a strong pause in the middle, sometimes chanted and sometimes spoken. The extended choral passages employed more intricate and variable meters and also involved both singing and dancing. The script indicates speakers but includes no stage directions; the action has to be deduced from the words of the text and is sometimes a matter of scholarly debate. We are missing the actors' costumes and gestures, the notes of the Chorus's songs, and the steps of their dances. The text that remains offers us an opportunity to appreciate the verbal skill with which Euripides presents the strained relations and personal dilemmas of his characters and to imagine the full performance of which it forms only a part.

A Note on the Translation

One of my main goals for this translation has been to make the characters sound like real people. Greek tragedy is by our standards a formal and stylized medium, composed in verse and combining dialogue with episodes of choral song and dance that recall tragedy's origins in nondramatic forms of storytelling. The language of tragedy is shaped by many types of formalized speech, from the laments for the dead that were performed chiefly by women, to the legal and political rhetoric with which men pursued their interests in the law courts and the citizen assembly, to the densely metaphoric and allusive language of the poetic tradition. But tragedy is also drama, a new and sensational form for its first audiences, in which figures from mythology speak to each other directly in real time. Euripides, whose *Medea* was probably written about a century after tragedy's earliest beginnings, was especially known for making those mythological figures feel contemporary. The comic poet Aristophanes depicts him as boasting that he "democratized" tragedy and put it on a diet, freeing it from high-flown poetic diction. So in working with Euripides it seemed especially important to avoid the stilted or stagy quality that hampers many translations of tragedy. This is often due to the translator sticking too closely to the exact wording of the original, vainly hoping to give readers the same experience they themselves have when reading the Greek text. I have tried instead to find the small shifts and adjustments that allow the sense of the original to come through in words that a current English speaker might actually say.

Some of the most challenging passages from this perspective are the wordless cries that tragic circumstances regularly elicit from the characters; these can sound so alien to present-day audiences that they demand translation into something less literal. My solution is to make those characters put their feelings into words. When Medea prefaces a wish to die with *iō moi moi*, "oh my, oh my," I have her say instead, "I can't take any more" (97); when her concerned Nurse reacts with an *iō moi moi* of her own, I have her say, "No, no! I don't like the sound of that" (115). Medea's contemptuous outburst when Jason explains that his desertion of her is actually to her advantage—literally, "O entirely evil one!"—can come across as bombastic and artificial, so I have chosen to rephrase it as "You really are disgusting!" (465). When Medea talks the Corinthian king Creon into postponing her exile just long enough for her to destroy him, he explains his decision in terms that are natural in Greek but strained in English: "In no way is my temper tyrannical by nature"; I have him say instead, "I'm really not a tyrant at heart" (348). These characters' words may be divided into lines of verse and their speeches may be long and declamatory, but Euripides still manages to make us witness the cruel sparring of an estranged couple and hear the complacent self-regard that blinds men like Jason and Creon to Medea's plots, and those accents need to come through in translation.

At the same time, this is a translation, not an adaptation, and my departures from the original wording are always minimal. I also keep to the same number of lines as are found in the Greek text, and seek to preserve through the distinctive register and rhythms of the choral passages the important difference between spoken dialogue and song accompanied by dance. This closeness to the original is essential if the translation is going to provide its readers with a version of Euripides' play that gives an authentic sense of what the original is like, both for its own sake and as a basis for appreciating the many creative adaptations of Euripides'

Medea they may encounter. *Medea* is one of the classical Greek tragedies that has been most often reworked by modern writers in order to dramatize concerns that arise from their own particular time and place: to choose just one timely example, Luis Alfaro's *Mojada: A Medea in Los Angeles,* developed over the period 2012–15, reimagines Medea as a Mexican immigrant to the United States. My translation needs to make clear in English what Euripides accomplished when he retold the Medea myth for his fifth-century B.C.E. Athenian contemporaries, in part so that modern readers can understand what a contemporary playwright like Alfaro is celebrating, building on, and transforming as he makes Euripides' play his own.

This translation is based on the Greek text in the edition of *Medea* for the Cambridge Greek and Latin Classics series by Donald Mastronarde, whose excellent commentary I have relied on throughout. I have also benefited from the edition and commentary by Judith Mossman in the Aris & Phillips Classical Texts series.

Euripides

Medea

I've done what I had to: I've pierced your heart. (1360)

τῆς σῆς γὰρ ὡς χρῆν καρδίας ἀνθηψάμην.

Characters

MEDEA

JASON

MEDEA'S NURSE

TUTOR OF MEDEA AND JASON'S SONS

CREON, KING OF CORINTH

AEGEUS, KING OF ATHENS

MESSENGER

CHORUS OF CORINTHIAN WOMEN

MEDEA AND JASON'S TWO SONS

Attendants

Medea

(Mēdeia)

First produced in 431 B.C.E.

(The setting is Corinth, in front of the house in which Medea and Jason have been living.)

(Enter Medea's Nurse from inside the house.)

NURSE
  If only the *Argo* had not slipped through
  the dark Clashing Rocks and landed at Colchis,
  if only that pine tree had not been cut down
  high on Mount Pelion and made into oars
  for the heroes who went out for the Golden Fleece,
  sent by King Pelias. Then my mistress Medea
  would never have sailed to the towers of Iolcus,
  overwhelmed by her love for Jason.
  She would not have talked the daughters of Pelias
  into killing their father, then fled here to Corinth   10
  with her husband and sons—where even in exile
  she has charmed the citizens of her new home,
  doing whatever she could to help out Jason.
  That is the strongest safeguard there is:
  when a wife always sides with her husband.
  But now they're at odds, their bond is infected.
  Deserting his children along with my mistress,
  Jason has climbed into a royal bed,
  with the daughter of Creon, king of this land.
  Poor Medea feels cruelly dishonored: 20
  she keeps shouting about their oaths and bringing up
  the solemn pledge of their joined right hands;
  she keeps calling on the gods to witness
  what kind of thanks she gets from Jason.
  She stays in bed and won't eat; she hurts all over.
  She's been weeping constantly since she heard

that she has been cast off by her husband.
She stares at the ground. When friends give advice,
she listens no more than a stone or the sea,
though sometimes she turns her pale neck away,   30
and sighs to herself about her dear father,
her homeland, her house—all those she betrayed
when she left with the man who now rejects her.
Poor thing, this disaster has made her learn
how hard it is to be cut off from home.
She hates her sons, gets no joy from seeing them.
I am afraid that she's planning something
[I know her: she's relentless and will not put up
with being mistreated. I can imagine
her sharpening a knife and stabbing someone,   40
sneaking into the house where the wedding bed's made,
to kill the king and his daughter's new bridegroom]°
and will only cause herself more trouble.
She is fierce. If you get into a fight with her,
you won't come out singing a victory song.

(*Enter the Tutor with Medea's Two Sons.*)

But here are the boys coming back from their run,
not thinking about their mother's problems—
young minds don't like to dwell on trouble.

TUTOR

Old servant of my mistress's house,
why do you stand here alone by the door,   50
pouring out your troubles to yourself?
Surely Medea doesn't want you to leave her?

NURSE

Old tutor of the sons of Jason,
when slaves are true-hearted, if their masters' luck
takes a turn for the worse, they suffer too.
I felt so wretched about my mistress
that I craved the relief of coming out here
to tell her sad story to heaven and earth.

TUTOR
  That poor woman has not stopped lamenting?

NURSE
  If only! Her pain's still in its early stages.   60

TUTOR
  What a fool, even if she is my mistress!
  She still doesn't know her latest troubles.

NURSE
  What is it, old man? Don't keep it to yourself.

TUTOR
  No, nothing. I shouldn't have said what I did.

NURSE
  Please don't leave a fellow slave in the dark.
  If it really matters, I won't tell anyone.

TUTOR
  I heard someone talking, though he didn't notice.
  I was watching the old men playing checkers
  there where they sit by the spring of Peirene.
  He said that Creon, the king here in Corinth,   70
  is planning to exile these boys from the city,
  with their mother. I have no idea
  if this is true. I certainly hope not.

NURSE
  Would Jason really put his sons through that,
  even if he is on bad terms with their mother?

TUTOR
  Old loyalties are trumped by new ones;
  and that man is no friend to this household.

NURSE

We're done for if we face a new wave of troubles
when we haven't bailed ourselves out from the last.

TUTOR

But now's not the right time for her to find out.   80
So you should keep quiet. Don't say a word.

NURSE

Children, do you hear how your father treats you?
He is my master: I can't curse him. But—
it's clear he's willing to hurt his own family.

TUTOR

And who isn't? It should be plain to you
that all people put themselves before others
[sometimes with good reason, sometimes for gain]
if this father prefers his new wife to his children.

NURSE

Go inside, boys. It will all be fine.
Now you, make sure they are kept by themselves,   90
not near their mother while she's so distraught.
She looks at them the way a mad bull would,
as if she's about to make some move.
She won't stop raging until she crushes someone—
better her enemies than people she loves.

MEDEA (*from inside*)

It's too much, too much to bear!
I can't take any more. I want to die!

NURSE

Boys, see what I mean! Your mother
keeps stirring up her angry heart.
Quickly, quickly, into the house,   100
but don't go near her: stay out of view.

Don't get too close, be on the watch
for her vengeful heart and her self-willed,
savage temper.
Go on inside, quick as you can.
Her grief is like a thundercloud
which her mounting fury will ignite.
And then what will she do,
this proud-to-the-core, uncurbable spirit
stung by sorrows?   110

(*Exit the Tutor and Medea's Two Sons into the house.*)

MEDEA
I've been hurt, I've been hurt, that's why I cry.
Boys, you are cursed, your mother is loathsome.
You might as well die along with your father.
Let the whole house come down!

NURSE
No, no! I don't like the sound of that.
Why blame your sons for their father's
offenses? Why turn on them?
Children, I'm sick with fear for you.
Our rulers have frightening tempers;
rarely governed, always in charge,   120
they can't let go of their anger.
Better to stay on a level plain.
I'd rather grow old in safety
and not lead a life of grandeur.
"Moderation" is a fine motto,
and we do well to live by it.
Reaching for more never brings
any real advantage in human life—
only greater ruin when an angry god
comes down on a house.   130

(*Enter the Chorus of Corinthian Women.*)

CHORUS

I heard a voice! I heard the cry
of that poor Colchian woman!
Tell us, old nurse, has she still not calmed down?
I'm sure I could hear through the double doors   134-35°
her wailing voice.
I get no joy from the grief in this house.
I consider myself a friend.

NURSE

There is no house. That's all gone.
The husband's possessed by a royal bed.   140
The wife wastes away in the innermost room,
and will not be comforted
by anything a friend can say.

MEDEA

Let it come! A thunderbolt
straight through my head!
Why be alive? In death
I can rest from a life I hate.

CHORUS

O Zeus, O Earth, O Light!
Do you hear the grief
in that girl's sad song?°   150
Why this foolish lust
for a fatal resting place?
You want death to hurry up?
Do not ever ask for that.
So your husband adores someone else.
You should not rage at him.
Zeus will stand up for you.
Do not ruin yourself mourning that man.   158-59

MEDEA

Mighty Themis! Holy Artemis!°   160
Do you see what I suffer—even after

I bound my hateful husband with solemn oaths?
I'd gladly watch him and his new bride
being smashed to bits with their whole house
for the huge wrong they have done to me.
My father! My city!—shamefully lost
when I killed my brother.

NURSE

You can hear what gods she calls on:
unfailing Themis and great Zeus,
who oversees the oaths of mortals.   170
There is no way she'll end her anger
with just some empty gesture.

CHORUS

If she would meet us
face-to-face
and listen to our words,
she might let go of the rage in her heart,
and soften her harsh temper.
I am always eager
to help a friend.
Go bring her out of the house.   180
Tell her we're on her side.
You have to act before she can hurt
those boys in there: grief spurs her on.

NURSE

I doubt I can persuade her,
but I'll do as you ask me to,
and make one last attempt.
When we try to speak to her,
she glares at us like a bull
or a lioness with newborn cubs.
I have to say our ancestors   190
showed very little sense
when they invented melodies
for revels, festivals, and feasts,

the sweetest sounds in life,
but made no songs or harmonies
to soothe the bitter grief
that leads to death and devastation
and brings whole houses down.
A musical cure for that would be
worth having. Why should people sing   200
when they're gathered at a feast
and there's joy enough already
in the meal's abundance?

(*Exit the Nurse into the house.*)

CHORUS
  I hear the pain in her loud laments;
  she shouts out high and shrill,
  at the faithless husband who spurns her bed.
  She calls on Themis to hear her wrongs,
  daughter of Zeus, upholder of oaths.   208–09
  Because of an oath, she crossed to Greece,   210
  sailing on the dark night waves   211–12
  of the Black Sea's watery gate.

(*Enter Medea from the house, with attendants.*)

MEDEA
  Women of Corinth, I have left the house
  to avoid offending you. With many people,
  you know that they're proud whether they stay home
  or go out. But others are seen as aloof
  just because they choose to lead quiet lives.
  People aren't fair when they judge with their eyes.
  Not taking the trouble to look inside,   220
  they hate someone on sight who's done them no harm.
  So a stranger really has to fit in.
  It's not good when even a self-willed native
  is out of touch and rude to fellow citizens.
  In my case, this unexpected calamity
  has crushed my spirit. I am finished, friends,

done with life's joys. I wish I was dead.
My husband, who was everything to me,
is actually, I now see, the worst of men.
Of all living, breathing, thinking creatures   230
women are the most absolutely wretched.
First, you have to pay an enormous sum
to buy a husband° who, to make things worse,
gets to be the master of your body.
And it's a gamble: you're as likely to get
a bad one as a good one. Divorce means disgrace
for women, and you can't say no to a husband.
Finding herself among strange laws and customs,
a wife needs to be clairvoyant; she has not
learned at home how to deal with her mate.   240
If we work hard at all these things,
and our husbands don't chafe at the yoke,
that's an enviable life. If not, we're better off dead.
A man who feels oppressed by the company at home
goes out and gets relief for his low spirits,
[turning to a friend or someone else his age,]
but we can only look to that one other person.
They tell us that we enjoy a sheltered life,
staying at home while they are out fighting.
How wrong they are! I would rather face battle   250
three times than go through childbirth once.
But it isn't the same for you as for me.
This is your city. The houses you grew up in,
all your daily pleasures, your friends, are here.
I am alone, without a city, disowned
by my husband, snatched from a foreign land.
I have no mother, brother, or other family
to shelter me now that disaster has struck.
So I have just one thing to ask of you:
if some plan or scheme occurs to me   260
by which I can get back at my husband
[and the king and his daughter, Jason's new wife],
say nothing. A woman is usually quite timid,
shying away from battles and weapons,

but if her marriage bed's dishonored,
no one has a deadlier heart.

CHORUS

I will do that. You are right to pay him back,
Medea. I can see why you're aggrieved.

(*Enter Creon.*)

But here is Creon, ruler of this land,
coming to announce some new decision.   270

CREON

You, with your scowls and your spite for your husband,
Medea, I command you to leave this land.
Take your two sons and go into exile—
and no delaying. I have the authority
to make this decree, and I'm not going home
until I've placed you outside our borders.

MEDEA

Oh no! I am completely destroyed.
My enemies are spreading their sails to the wind,
and I can't disembark from disaster.
But bad as things are, I have to ask: 280
what's your reason, Creon, for throwing me out?

CREON

I'll come right out and say it: I'm afraid
that you'll do my daughter incurable harm.
There are many signs that point to this.
You are clever and skilled at causing damage,
and you feel injured in your empty bed.
People have told me you're threatening us all:
the bride's father, the bridegroom, and the bride.
So I'm acting first to protect myself.
I would rather earn your hatred now   290
than regret later on that I was too lenient.

MEDEA

Not again!
Creon, the same thing keeps happening:
my reputation gets me into trouble.
No man who has his wits about him
would raise his sons to be too clever.
Not only will they be considered lazy,
·they'll be resented by their fellow citizens.
When you propose a clever plan to dullards,
they see you as useless rather than clever;
and those who are thought to be sophisticated   300
are bothered when the people think you're smarter.
This is exactly what has happened to me.
I'm clever, so I'm envied by one group
[to some I'm idle, to some the reverse]
and annoy the rest—cleverness has limits.
I know you're afraid I'll do you some harm.
But why be worried? I am in no position
to go on the offensive against a king.
How have you wronged me? You gave your daughter
to the man you wanted to. The one I hate   310
is my husband. You were acting sensibly.
I don't blame you because you're doing well.
Marry her off! Best of luck to all! But—
just let me stay. I may have been mistreated,
but I'll keep quiet, yielding to my betters.

CREON

Your words sound pleasing, but I am afraid
that you have some evil plan in your heart.
In fact, I trust you less than I did before.
A hot-tempered woman—or man—is easier
to guard against than a silent, clever one.   320
No, you have to leave at once. Enough talking.
It is decided: you are my enemy,
and none of your tricks can keep you here.

(*Medea kneels and grasps Creon's knees and hand in a gesture of ritual supplication.*)

MEDEA
No! By your knees! By your daughter, the bride!

CREON
Your words are wasted. You will never convince me.

MEDEA
You're ignoring my prayers and driving me out?

CREON
I care about my family, not about you.

MEDEA
My lost home! I can't stop thinking about it.

CREON
That's what means most to me, after my children.

MEDEA
Oh, what a disaster to fall in love!　　　　　330

CREON
That depends, I'd say, on the circumstances.

MEDEA
Zeus, be sure to notice who's making me suffer.

CREON
Don't be a fool! Go, and take my troubles with you.

MEDEA
I have troubles too, far more than I need.

CREON
My guards are preparing to throw you out.

MEDEA
No, not that! Creon, I implore you.

CREON
So you're determined to make this difficult.

MEDEA
I will leave. I don't ask you to change that.

CREON
Then why keep pressing me? Let go of my hand.

MEDEA
Just let me stay here for one more day   340
so I can work out my plans for exile
and make some arrangements for my sons,
since their father is not inclined to help.
Show them some pity. You have children yourself;
it's only natural to wish these boys well.
I'm not worried about exile for myself
but I feel the hardship it brings my sons.

CREON
I'm really not a tyrant at heart:
to my own cost, I have listened to others.
Even though I know it's not a good idea,   350
you get your wish. But I warn you,
if tomorrow's sun finds you and your boys
still inside the borders of this country,
you will die. I say it, and I mean it.
So stay on, if you must, for this one day;
you won't have time to do the harm I fear.

(*Exit Creon. Medea stands up.*)

CHORUS
Poor, poor woman,
weighed down by troubles,

where can you turn? What welcome,
what house, what sheltering land   360
[will you find]?
Medea, some god has tossed you
into a sea of constant trials.

MEDEA
It's bad all around. Who would deny that?
But don't imagine that everything's settled.
There are struggles ahead for the bridal pair,
and many ordeals for the bride's father.
Would I have fawned on him like that
without something to gain or a secret plan?
There wouldn't have been that talking and touching.   370
But he is such a credulous fool:
when he had a chance to throw me out
and foil my plans, he gave me one more day
to make corpses out of my three tormenters—
the father, the daughter, and my own husband.
I can think of many routes to their death;
I'm not sure, friends, which one to try first,
whether to set the newlyweds' house on fire,
or stab someone's liver with a sharpened sword,
silently entering the bridal bedroom.   380
But there is a risk: if I am caught
sneaking into the house, I will lose my life
and give my enemies a chance to laugh.
The safest course is the one I know best:
to poison them with deadly drugs.
That's it then.
But once they are dead—then what city
will take me in? Where is the friend
who will save my life by giving me shelter?
Nowhere. So I will wait a little while,
and if some tower of safety appears   390
I will kill them with a hidden trick.
But if I am forced to act in the open,

I will strike with a sword. Ready to die,
I will go to the very edge of daring.
By Hecate,° whom I most revere,
the goddess who is my chosen ally,
who haunts the darkest corners of my house,
they will not get away with causing this pain.
I will make sure they find their marriage bitter,
and bitter the tie with Creon, bitter my exile.   400
Now Medea, use everything you know;
you must plot and scheme as you approach
the dreadful act that will test your spirit.
Do you see what is being done to you?
Do not be mocked by this Sisyphean wedding;°
you spring from a noble father and Helios the sun.
You have the skill, and along with that
a woman's nature—useless for doing good
but just right for contriving evil.

CHORUS
Sacred streams are flowing backwards;   410–11
right and wrong are turned around.
It's men who do the shady scheming,
swear by the gods, then break their oaths.
News of this will bring us glory,   415–16
rightful honor for the female race;   417–18
women will at last be free
from the taint of ugly rumors.   420

Enough of ancient poets' legends
that tell of us as breaking faith!
The lord of song, divine Apollo,
did not grant the lyre's sweet music
for the speaking of our minds,
or I could have made an answer   426–27
to the stories spread by men.   428–29
Time's long record speaks on both sides.   430–31

Mad with love, you left your father.
Sailing through the briny border
of the double Clashing Rocks,
you settled in a land of strangers.
Now your husband's left your bed;
so you're banished from this country,
a lonely exile without rights.

All over Greece, oaths prove hollow;
shame has melted into air.   440
And for you there's no safe harbor
in your lost paternal home,
no escaping from your troubles,
as you watch a royal princess
take your marriage and your house.

(*Enter Jason.*)

JASON
This is not the first time that I've observed
how impossible a stubborn person can be.
You had the chance to stay in this country,
going along with what your betters had planned,
but you're being thrown out for your pointless rants,   450
and there's nothing I can do. Fine! Don't stop
talking about "that disgusting Jason."
But for what you've said about the rulers—
you are lucky that it's only exile.
The king gets more and more angry. I've tried
to calm him down, hoping you could stay.
Yet you keep up this nonsense, raving on
against the king. So you're being thrown out.
Still, I am not one to abandon family.
I'm here now to look out for your interests,   460
so you and the boys don't leave without money
or other provisions. Exile's not easy.
Maybe you can't stop hating me,
but I'll always want what is best for you.

MEDEA
You really are disgusting! That sums up
what I have to say about your spinelessness.
You've really come here, when you are hated
[by me and the gods and everyone else]?
It's not some daring, noble endeavor
to look friends in the face after you've wronged them,   470
but the lowest and sickest of human failings:
shamelessness. Still, it is good that you came.
If I name all your appalling actions,
I'll get some relief, and you'll feel much worse.
Let me start at the very beginning:
I saved you, as every Greek knows
who shipped out with you on the *Argo*,
when you had to bring the fire-breathing bulls
under a yoke and sow a deadly field.
And that serpent, which never slept   480
and held the Golden Fleece in winding coils,
I killed it, bringing you the light of salvation.
And as for me, I cheated my father
and followed you to Iolcus and Mount Pelion,
infatuated, not thinking straight.
I made Pelias die in the most gruesome way,
at his daughters' hands; I ruined his house.
All of this I did for you, you lowlife,
and you have deserted me for someone new
even though we have children. If we didn't,   490
you could be forgiven for wanting her.
Our oaths mean nothing to you. I can't tell
if you think those gods have lost their power,
or imagine that the rules have changed for mortals—
since you're well aware that you broke a promise.
My right hand here—to think I let you touch it,
and to clasp my knees. I was abused
by a swindler, deceived by false hopes.
Still, let me ask you for some friendly advice.
(But why should I think you'd help me now?   500
Well, if I ask you, it'll make you look worse.)

So where should I go? To my father's house,
which I betrayed when I ran off with you?
To the poor daughters of Pelias? I'm sure
I'd be welcome there, where I killed their father.
That is how it stands: my friends at home
hate me now, and those I should have treated well
I turned into enemies by helping you.
For what I did, you made me the envy
of all Greek women—with such a marvelous catch,   510
such a loyal husband that I'm being expelled,
a miserable outcast, from this country,
without any friends, alone with my sons.
It doesn't look so good for the bridegroom—
children out begging with the woman who saved him.
Zeus, you should have given us a touchstone
for human nature as you did for gold!
We need a way to tell from someone's looks
whether or not he's base on the inside.

CHORUS

There is a dreadful, incurable anger   520
when former lovers fall to fighting.

JASON

It seems I'll have to be a skillful speaker
and, like a careful pilot, reef in my sails
if I have any hope of outrunning
the surging onslaught of your angry words.
You make much of the help you gave me,
but I say that it was Aphrodite° alone
who assured the success of my venture.
You may be quick-witted, but like it or not,
I could tell how the sure darts of Eros   530
were what compelled you to save my life.
But no need to tally this up exactly:
whatever you did was helpful enough.
Still, it's my view that you got much more
out of my being saved than I ever did.

First of all, you are living in Greece,
not some foreign country. Here you find justice
and the rule of law; force has no standing.
And all of Greece knows how clever you are;
you're famous. If you lived at the ends of the earth,   540
no one would ever have heard of you.
I see no point in a house full of gold,
or a gift for singing better than Orpheus,°
without the good fortune of being well known.
So—since you have turned this into a contest,
those are the things I accomplished for you.
Now, on this royal marriage that you dislike,
I can show you that I acted wisely,
soberly, and in the best interests
of you and the boys. Just stay calm for a moment.   550
When I moved here from the city of Iolcus,
I was dragged down by impossible problems.
What better solution could there be
for an exile like me than to marry the princess?
You are upset, but it's not what you think,
that I'm sick of you and smitten with this girl,
or want some prize for having lots of children;
I am satisfied with the ones we've got.
It's so we'll live well and won't be in need.
And that is important. I can tell you: 560
everyone steers clear of a penniless friend.
I will raise our sons as befits our family
and add some brothers to the boys you gave me.
Bringing them together in a single tribe,
I'll prosper. What are more children to you?
In my case, having new offspring benefits
the older ones. Is that such a bad plan?
You wouldn't say so if it weren't for the sex.
You women reach the point where you think
if all's well in the bedroom everything's fine;   570
but if some trouble arises there,
you insist on rejecting whatever's best.
We should have some other way of getting children.

Then there would be no female race,
and mankind would be free from trouble.

CHORUS

Jason, you've put together a polished speech.
But, at the risk of disagreeing, I say
that you do wrong to desert your wife.

MEDEA

I'm clearly different from everyone else.
To me, a scoundrel who is good at speaking   580
should have to pay a special price for that.
Since he knows he can gloss over his crimes,
he'll try anything, though cleverness has limits.
That's what you are. So don't try to impress me
with clever words. A single point refutes you:
if you were so noble, you would have gotten
my consent to this marriage, not kept it secret.

JASON

Oh yes, I'm sure you would have agreed
if I had told you then, when even now
you can't help reacting with fury.   590

MEDEA

That wasn't it. You thought a foreign wife
would be an embarrassment in years to come.

JASON

You need to understand. It is not for the woman
that I'm taking on this royal marriage.
It's what I told you before: I only want
to give you protection and safeguard our children
by fathering royal siblings for them.

MEDEA

Spare me a life of shameful wealth
or a good situation that eats at my soul.

JASON

You know what you really need to pray for?   600
The sense not to see a good thing as shameful,
not to think you're suffering when you're doing fine.

MEDEA

Go on, be cruel. You have a safe home here,
while I'll be cast out with nowhere to go.

JASON

You chose that. Don't blame anyone else.

MEDEA

How? I betrayed you by marrying somebody?

JASON

By rudely cursing the royal family.

MEDEA

Well, I'll bring a curse to your house too.

JASON

I have had enough of squabbling with you,
but if you want some money from me   610
to provide for you and the boys in exile,
just say so. I want to be generous
and can contact friends who will treat you well.
You would be an idiot to turn me down.
You'll be better off if you forget your anger.

MEDEA

I want nothing to do with your friends.
I won't take anything you give. Don't bother.
No good comes from a bad man's gifts.

JASON

Well, the gods will witness how eager I am
to do what I can for you and the boys.   620

You are so stubborn that you reject what's good
and snub your friends. You will suffer all the more.

MEDEA

Just go! I'm sure that staying away this long
has left you longing for your new bride.
Go play the groom. And maybe I'm right to hope
you will have a marriage that makes you weep.

(*Exit Jason.*)

CHORUS

Overwhelming love never leads to virtue,   627–28
    or a good reputation.   629–30
Just enough Aphrodite is the greatest blessing.   631–32
Goddess, don't aim at me with your golden bow   633–34
    and arrows dipped in desire.

I choose to be wooed by sober restraint,
    best gift of the gods.
I won't have Aphrodite stirring up quarrels,   638–39
by making me fall for a stranger. She should grant us   640–42
    harmonious marriages.   643–44

Beloved country! Beloved home!
May I never lose my city;
that is a life without hope,   647–48
the hardest of trials to bear.
Better, far better to die,   650
than ever come to that.
There is no deeper pain
than being cut off from home.

I have seen it for myself;
no one had to tell me.
For you have no city,
no friends who feel for you
in your bitter struggles.

One who does not honor friends
with an open heart, 660
deserves an awful death
and is no friend of mine.

(*Enter* AEGEUS.)

AEGEUS
Hello, Medea! And all good wishes—
the warmest of greetings among true friends.

MEDEA
Good wishes to you, son of wise Pandion,
Aegeus! Where are you coming from?

AEGEUS
Straight from Apollo's ancient oracle.

MEDEA
What took you there, to the center of the earth?

AEGEUS
I wanted to know how I might have children.

MEDEA
Goodness! Have you been childless all this time? 670

AEGEUS
Yes, childless—thanks, I am sure, to some god.

MEDEA
Do you have a wife, or do you sleep alone?

AEGEUS
I'm married; I have a wife who shares my bed.

MEDEA
And what did Apollo say about children?

AEGEUS

Subtler words than a man can make sense of.

MEDEA

Am I allowed to know what he said?

AEGEUS

Of course. I need the help of your clever mind.

MEDEA

Then if it's allowed, tell me what he said.

AEGEUS

Not to untie the foot of the wineskin . . . °

MEDEA

Before doing what? Or arriving where?   680

AEGEUS

Before I get back to my ancestral hearth.

MEDEA

And what's your reason for landing here?

AEGEUS

There's a man called Pittheus, king of Troezen.

MEDEA

Son of Pelops, said to be very pious.

AEGEUS

I want to ask him about the prophecy.

MEDEA

Yes, he's wise and knows about such things.

AEGEUS

And he's my most trusted comrade at war.

MEDEA
Well, good luck! I hope you get what you want.

AEGEUS
But why are you so red-eyed and pale?

MEDEA
It turns out I have the worst possible husband.   690

AEGEUS
What are you saying? Tell me what's upset you.

MEDEA
Jason mistreats me though I've given him no cause.

AEGEUS
What is he doing? Explain what you mean.

MEDEA
He put another woman in charge of our house.

AEGEUS
Would he do something so improper?

MEDEA
He would. So I, once prized, am now dismissed.

AEGEUS
Is he in love? Or has he fallen out with you?

MEDEA
So much in love that he's abandoned his family.

AEGEUS
Well, if he's that bad, forget about him.

MEDEA
He's in love with the thought of a royal match.   700

AEGEUS

Then tell me: who is the new wife's father?

MEDEA

Creon, who rules right here in Corinth.

AEGEUS

Well, I can see why you are angry.

MEDEA

Devastated. And I'm being expelled.

AEGEUS

From bad to worse! What's the reason for that?

MEDEA

Creon has declared me an exile from Corinth.

AEGEUS

And Jason accepts this? That's not right.

MEDEA

He protests now, but he'll gladly put up with it.
So I'm reaching out my hands to your face
and making myself your suppliant.   710
Take pity on me in my wretched state,
don't let me become a lonely outcast.
Take me into your country and your house.
Do this, and may the gods grant your wish.
May you live out the happy life you long for.
You don't know how lucky you are to find me:
I can take care of your lack of children.
I know the right drugs to make you a father.

AEGEUS

There are many reasons why I want to help.
First the gods, who favor suppliants,   720

and then the children you say I could have—
something where I'm really at a loss.
So, if you can get yourself to my land,
I will try to give you proper shelter.
[I should make one thing plain to you:
I'm not willing to take you away from here.]
If you leave this place on your own
and arrive at my house, also on your own,
you will be safe. I will not hand you over.
But I can't offend my friends while I'm here.   730

MEDEA

Agreed. Now if you could make a formal pledge,
then I will feel you've treated me perfectly.

AEGEUS

You don't trust me? What's on your mind?

MEDEA

I trust you. But Pelias's family hates me,
and Creon too. If you are bound by oaths,
you can't let them take me from your land.
If you just say yes and don't swear by the gods,
you might end up being gracious and giving in
to their demands. I'm completely powerless,
while they have wealth and status on their side.   740

AEGEUS

You clearly have this all figured out.
So if you think I should, I won't refuse.
This will put me in a stronger position,
with a good excuse to give your enemies,
and it helps you. Name the gods I should swear by.

MEDEA

Swear by the Earth and by the Sun, father
of my father, and the entire race of gods.

AEGEUS

To do—or not to do—what? Say it.

MEDEA

Not ever to cast me out from your land,
and if some enemy tries to lead me away,   750
not to allow it while you live and breathe.

AEGEUS

I swear by the Earth and the light of the Sun,
and all the gods, I will do as you say.

MEDEA

Good. And the penalty if you break the oath?

AEGEUS

Whatever ungodly people have to suffer.

MEDEA

A good journey to you. All is in place.
I will come to your city as soon as I can,
once I have fulfilled my plans and desires.

CHORUS

May Hermes, guide of travelers,
speed you to your home,   760
and may you gain your heart's desire,
for you are an honorable man, Aegeus,
that is clear to me.

(*Exit Aegeus.*)

MEDEA

O Zeus, O Justice born of Zeus, O Sun!
Now, friends, I know I am on the path
to glorious victory over my enemies.
Now I feel sure they will have to pay.
I was at a loss, and then this man appeared,

who will be a safe haven when my plots are done.
I can fasten my mooring line to him   770
when I have made my way to Athens.
And now I will tell you what I have in mind;
listen to this, though I doubt you will like it.
I will send a trusted servant to Jason
who will ask him to meet me face-to-face.
When he comes, I will give a soothing speech
about how I agree with him and now believe
that his faithless marriage is a first-rate plan,
advantageous and well thought through.
Then I'll plead for the children to stay behind;   780
not that I want to leave them in this hostile land
[and have my children mistreated by enemies];
it's part of a trick to kill the king's daughter.
I'll send them to her with gifts in their hands
[for the bride, so they won't have to leave],
a delicate robe and a golden crown.
Once she takes this finery and puts it on,
she—and whoever touches her—will die
because of poisons I will spread on the gifts.
That's all there is to say on that subject.   790
But the thought of what I have to do next
fills me with grief: I need to kill the children,
no one should hope to spare them that.
Once I've torn Jason's house apart, I'll leave
and pay no price for the poor boys' death.
I will bring myself to this unholy act
because I cannot let my enemies laugh.
[So be it! Why should I live? I have no country,
no home, no way of escaping my troubles.]
It was a bad mistake to leave my home,   800
swayed by the words of a man from Greece,
but with the gods' help I will punish him.
He won't see the children we had grow up,
and he won't be able to have any more
with his brand-new bride: no, she's doomed
to an agonizing death from my drugs.

No one should think I am meek and mild
or passive. I am quite the opposite:
harsh to enemies and loyal to friends,
the kind of person whose life has glory.   810

CHORUS

Now that you have shared this plan with me,
I want to help you and to honor human law,
and so I say to you: don't do this thing.

MEDEA

I see why you say that, but there's no other way;
you haven't been through the troubles I have.

CHORUS

You would be able to kill your own children?

MEDEA

It is the surest way to wound my husband.

CHORUS

And to make yourself impossibly wretched.

MEDEA

So be it. We have done enough talking.

(*Medea turns to her attendants.*)

One of you servants, go bring Jason here.   820
And you, the friends I trust with my closest secrets,
if you respect me and have women's hearts,
you will say nothing about my plan.

(*Exit one of Medea's attendants.*)

CHORUS

The sons of Erectheus,° long blessed with wealth,
Athenian offspring of the Olympian gods,

raised in a land untouched by war,   826–27
nourished by the glorious arts,   828–29
stride easily through the radiant air,   830–31
where once, it's said, the holy Muses   832–33
gave birth to golden Harmony.

I've heard that Aphrodite dips her cup
in the streams of clear Cephisus,°
and sends sweet breezes through the land.   837–38
Crowned with a twining garland   839–40
of fragrant, blooming roses,   841–42
she sets Desire at Wisdom's side   843–44
to foster all that's good.

How can that land of sacred streams,
that open-hearted city,
be a fitting home for you,
unholy woman,
killer of children?   850
Think what it is to strike a child!
Think who you are killing!
By every sacred thing
I beg of you:
spare those boys.

How can you find the will,
how can you steel your mind,
to lift your hand against your sons,
to do this awful thing?
How will you stop your tears   860
when you see them dying?
They will huddle at your knees,
and you will not be able
to spill their blood
with a steady heart.

(*Enter Jason.*)

JASON

    You called me, so I've come. You may hate me,
    but I won't let you down. I'm eager to hear
    what you think you may need from me after all.

MEDEA

    Jason, please overlook what I said before.
    You should be willing to put up with my fits,   870
    for the sake of the love that we once shared.
    And I have been thinking all of this over
    and berating myself for being obtuse.
    Why turn on those who wish me well,
    picking a fight with the country's rulers
    and my husband, who serves us all
    by marrying a princess and giving our sons
    new royal brothers? Why be angry?
    The gods will provide, so how can I lose?
    Shouldn't I think of the boys? I can't forget   880
    that I'm an exile and have no friends.
    When I look at it that way, I can see
    I've been confused and my rage was pointless.
    I'm all for it now. I think you are wise
    to arrange this connection. I'm the fool:
    I should have thrown myself into these plans
    and helped them along, tending the bed
    and gladly serving your new bride.
    It's just that women are . . . well, not quite wicked,
    but anyway you shouldn't copy us   890
    and get caught up in silly quarrels.
    Please forgive me: I was wrong before
    and now I understand much better.
    Come out of the house
    to greet your father and talk to him.

(*Enter the Tutor and Medea's Two Sons from the house.*)

    End your anger toward one you should love
    just as I, your mother, am doing.

We have made our peace, there is no more strife.
So take his hand. But oh, when I think
of all the trouble the future conceals!   900
My children, in your lives to come,
will you reach out a loving arm to me?
I am so quick to weep and full of fear.
I'm making up my quarrel with your father,
but even so my eyes are filled with tears.

CHORUS
Tears are coming to my eyes as well.
I only hope there's nothing worse ahead.

JASON
I'm pleased with your present behavior, Medea,
and I forgive the past: of course a woman minds
if her husband decides to import a new wife.   910
But now your feelings have turned around,
and you recognize the better course at last.
That shows you are a sensible woman.
Now boys, don't think I've been a negligent father.
With the gods' help, I've secured your position.
I am quite sure that you will be leaders
here in Corinth, you and your new siblings.
Just be strong and stay well. I will do the rest,
along with whatever god's on our side.
I hope to see you turning into fine young men,   920
and towering over my enemies.
But you, why are your cheeks covered with tears?
Why do you look pale and turn away?
Aren't you happy with what I am saying?

MEDEA
It's nothing—just the thought of these children.

JASON
Don't worry. I will take care of everything.

MEDEA

You're right. I can rely on your promises.
It's just that women are made for tears.

JASON

But why are you so sad about the children?

MEDEA

I am their mother. And your hopes for their future   930
filled me with fear that those things won't happen.
Now some of what you are here to discuss
has been settled, so I'll move on to the rest:
since the rulers have decided to banish me
(and I really do see that it's for the best
so I won't be in your way, or theirs,
since I can't help seeming antagonistic),
I will comply and leave the country.
But the boys should stay here and be raised by you;
ask Creon to spare them this exile.   940

JASON

I may not convince him, but I will try.

MEDEA

You should get your bride to ask her father
to let the boys stay here in this country.

JASON

Good idea. She'll do it if I ask her:
she is a woman like any other.

MEDEA

And I will be part of this effort too.
I will send her the most splendid gifts
that can be found anywhere in the world
[a delicate robe and a golden crown]
and the boys will take them. Now servants,   950
bring out the presents right away.

(*Exit an attendant into the house.*)

She will have many reasons to rejoice:
In you she has the best of husbands
and she will wear the ornaments
that my grandfather Helios left to his heirs.

(*Enter the attendant with the gifts.*)

Take these wedding presents, boys,
carry them to the happy royal bride.
They will be perfect gifts for her.

JASON

That's ridiculous! Don't deprive yourself.
Do you think the royal house needs dresses,   960
or gold? You should hold on to these things.
I am sure that her high regard for me
will matter more than material objects.

MEDEA

No. They say even the gods are moved by gifts.
For us, gold counts more than a million words.
Her fortunes are high, she has a god on her side,
she's young and has power. I'd give my life,
and not just gold, to save the boys from exile.
My sons, go into that fine rich house;
appeal to your father's new wife, my mistress;   970
ask for reprieve from a life of exile,
and hand her the gifts. It is essential
that she herself takes them from you.
Hurry! And bring back the good news
that you have made your mother's wish come true.

(*Exit Jason, Medea's Two Sons, and the Tutor.*)

CHORUS

No more hoping that those children will live.
No more, for they are on the road to murder.
The bride will reach out for the golden chains,

poor thing, she'll reach out for her doom.
With her own hands she will place in her hair   980–81
the finery of Death.

Lured by their lovely unearthly glow,
she'll put on the dress and the wrought-gold crown
and make her marriage in the world below.
That is the trap into which she will fall,
poor thing, she will follow her destiny,   987–88
inescapable Death.

And you, unlucky groom,   990
new member of the royal house,
you are not able to see
that you're leading your boys to their life's end,
and bringing a hateful death to your bride.
You have no idea of your fate.

And you, poor mother of these boys,
I also grieve for you,
since you are set on making them die
because of the bed which your husband left.
He thoughtlessly abandoned you   1000
and lives with another wife.

(*Enter Medea's Two Sons and the Tutor.*)

TUTOR
Mistress! The boys are spared the fate of exile!
The princess gladly accepted the gifts
with her own hands. She is on their side.
But . . .
why are you upset at this good fortune?
[Why have you turned your face away?
Why aren't you happy with what I'm saying?]

MEDEA
Oh no!

TUTOR
That doesn't fit with the news I brought.

MEDEA
Oh no, oh no!

TUTOR
What is it that I don't understand?
Was I wrong to think I was bringing good news?   1010

MEDEA
You bring the news you bring. It's not your fault.

TUTOR
But why are you crying and turning away?

MEDEA
I can't help it, old friend. Terrible plans
have been devised by the gods—and by me.

TUTOR
The boys' good standing here will bring you back.

MEDEA
First I, in my grief, will bring others down.

TUTOR
Other mothers have been torn from their children.
You are mortal and must accept misfortune.

MEDEA
Yes, yes, I will. Now you go inside.
Take care of whatever the boys might need.   1020

(*Exit the Tutor into the house.*)

O boys, boys, you still have a city,
and a home where, leaving me for good,
you will be cut off from your unhappy mother.

I will be an exile in a foreign land
without the delight of watching you thrive,
without the joy of preparing your weddings,
tending the bath and the bed, lifting the torches.
How much my own strong will has cost me!
I get nothing, boys, from raising you,
from running myself ragged with endless work.   1030
The birth pangs I endured were pointless.
It pains me to think what hopes I had
that you would care for me in old age
and prepare me for burial when I die—
the thing that everyone wants. But now
that happy dream is dead. Deprived of you,
I will live out my life in bitter grief.
And you will embark on a different life
with no more loving eyes for your mother.
But why, why, boys, are you looking at me?   1040
Why do you smile for this one last time?
Oh, what should I do? I lost heart, my friends,
as soon as I saw their beaming faces.
I can't do it. So much for my plans!
I will take the boys away from here.
Why make them suffer to hurt their father
if it means I suffer twice as much myself?
I can't do that. So much for my plans!
But wait! Can I really bear to be laughed at
and let my enemies go unpunished?   1050
I have to steel myself. I can't be weak
and let those tender thoughts take over.
Children, into the house. And anyone
who is out of place at my sacrifice
can stay away. I will not spare my hand.
But oh . . .
my angry heart, do not go through with this.
For all your pain, let the children live.
They can be with you and bring you joy.
And yet—by the vengeful spirits of deepest Hades—
there is no way I can allow my enemies   1060

to seize my children and to mistreat them.
[It is certain that they have to die. And so
I should kill them, since I gave them life.]
It is all in place: she cannot escape;
the crown is on her head; the royal bride
revels in her new dress. I heard it clearly.
Having set out myself on the darkest road,
I will send my sons down one that's even darker.
I will talk to them. Give me, my children,
give me, your mother, your hands to kiss.   1070
Oh this hand! this mouth! this face!
Oh my dear ones, my noble sons!
Be happy—but there. Your father wrecked
what we had here. Oh the joy of holding them,
of their tender skin, of their sweet breath.
Go in! Go in! I can no longer bear
to look at you. My grief is too strong.
I see the horror of what I am doing,
but anger overwhelms my second thoughts—°
anger, boundless source of evil.   1080

(*Exit Medea's Two Sons into the house.*)

CHORUS
I have often entered into
complicated trains of thought,
and pursued much deeper questions
than women are supposed to tackle.
For there's a Muse that favors me
and confers the gift of wisdom,
not on all, but on a few—
[you'll find some women here and there]
who are not strangers to that Muse.
So I can say that those who never   1090
find themselves producing children
are more fortunate by far
than those who do.
The childless never need to ask

whether children are, in the end,
a curse or blessing in human life;
and since they have none of their own,
they are spared a world of trouble.
Those parents who are blessed
with houses full of growing children
are constantly worn out by worry: 1100
will they be able to raise them well
and leave behind enough to live on?
And all along it isn't clear   1103
whether after all this care   1103A
they'll turn out well or badly.
Then there is one final drawback,
the hardest thing of all to bear:
when the parents find a way
to give their children what they need
to grow up strong and honest,
but then luck turns: death scoops them up   1110
and carries their bodies down to Hades.
What possible good can it do
for the gods to impose on us
this bitter, bitter sorrow
as the price of having children?

MEDEA
My friends, I have been waiting a long time now,
wondering how things would turn out in there.
But now I see one of Jason's servants
coming toward us. He is breathing hard,
and it's clear he has something grim to report.   1120

(*Enter the Messenger.*)

MESSENGER
[Oh you have done a dreadful, lawless thing]
Run, Medea! Run! Make your escape—
get away in a ship or overland in a carriage.

MEDEA

And what has happened that means I should flee?

MESSENGER

The royal princess has fallen down dead,
along with her father, because of your poison.

MEDEA

You have brought the most wonderful news.
I will always think of you as a true friend.

MESSENGER

What are you saying? Are you out of your mind?
You have desecrated the royal hearth,   1130
and you're glad? Not terrified at what you've done?

MEDEA

I have things to say in response to that.
But please do not rush through your report.
How exactly did they die? You will make me
twice as happy if they died horribly.

MESSENGER

When your boys and their father first arrived
at the new couple's house, there was great joy
among the household slaves. We had been worried,
but now a rumor was spreading through us
that you and Jason had patched up your quarrel.   1140
One kissed their hands, another their golden heads,
and I in my happiness followed along
into the women's rooms behind the children.
The lady who had become our new mistress
did not see at first that your sons were there;
she just gazed adoringly at Jason.
But then suddenly she shut her eyes
and turned her delicate face away,
disgusted by the children's presence.

But your husband calmed the girl down,   1150
saying, "They are family, don't reject them,
let your anger go, look this way again;
can't you treat your husband's kin as your own,
accept their gifts, and ask your father
to spare the boys from exile for my sake?"
She gave in when she saw those fine presents,
and granted him everything he asked.
As soon as the boys and their father had left,
she seized that elegant dress and put it on;
she placed the golden crown on her head   1160
and arranged her hair in a shining mirror,
smiling at her reflected features.
Then she jumped up from her chair and ran
all over the house on her little white feet,
delighted with her presents; she kept looking down
to see how the dress fell against her ankle.
But then we saw something truly horrible:
her color changed; she staggered sideways
on shaking legs; she nearly hit the ground
as she fell backward into a chair.   1170
An older woman, thinking at first
that she was possessed by some god like Pan,°
raised a shout of joy. But then she saw
the foaming mouth, the skin drained of blood,
the eyeballs twisting in their sockets.
She countered that shout of joy with a shriek
of woe. One slave girl rushed to the father's room;
another went straight to tell the husband
that his bride had collapsed. The whole house rang
with the sound of their frantic footsteps.   1180
In the time it would take a swift runner
to cover the last lap of a footrace,
she came out of her speechless, sightless trance
with an awful, chilling cry of pain.
She was under a double assault:
the golden crown she had put in her hair
spewed out a torrent of consuming flames,

while those fine robes she got from your boys
were eating away at her pale flesh.
Burning alive, she leapt up from her chair   1190
and shook her head from side to side,
trying to throw off the crown. But the bands
held tight, and all of her shaking
only made the fire blaze twice as high.
She gave up the struggle and fell to the floor.
Only a parent would have known who she was.
You really couldn't make out her eyes
or the shape of her face. From the top of her head
blood mixed with fire was streaming down;
the flesh flowed off her bones like pine sap,   1200
loosened by the fangs of your unseen poison,
a horrible sight. No one wanted to touch
the corpse. Her fate taught us caution.
But her poor father came in without warning;
he entered the room and found the body.
He began to wail and took it in his arms,
kissed it, and spoke to it: "My poor child,
what god has destroyed you in this cruel way,
making me lose you when I'm at death's door?
All I want is to die with you, dear child."   1210
When he stopped lamenting and tried to stand,
he got tangled up in those silky robes,
like a laurel shoot encircled by ivy.
It was a horrible sort of wrestling match:
he kept struggling to get up on his legs
while she held him back. He pulled hard
but the flesh just came off his old bones.
In the end, he stopped fighting for his life,
worn out, no longer equal to the ordeal.
Two corpses lie there, the girl and her father   1220
[nearby, a disaster that cries out for tears].
I won't go into what this means for you;
you'll find out what penalty you have to pay.
The old truth comes home to me again:
human life is an empty shadow.

People who believe themselves to be
the deepest thinkers are the biggest fools.
There isn't anyone who is truly blessed.
Rich people may be luckier than others
but I wouldn't really call them blessed.   1230

(*Exit the Messenger.*)

CHORUS
A god is giving Jason what he deserves:
trouble after trouble in a single day.
[Poor girl, poor daughter of Creon,
I feel for you: you have been sent
to Hades to pay for Jason's marriage.]

MEDEA
Friends! My plan is clear: as fast as I can
I will kill my sons and leave this land.
I cannot hold back and let those boys
be slaughtered by someone who loves them less.
They have to die, so it is only right   1240
that I who gave them life should kill them.
Arm yourself, my heart! Don't hesitate
to do the unavoidable awful thing.
I must pick up the sword and step across
the starting line of a painful course.
No weakening, no thoughts of the boys—
how sweet they are, how you gave them birth.
Forget your children for this one day;
grieve afterward. Even if you kill them,
they still are loved—by you, unlucky woman.   1250

(*Exit Medea into the house.*)

CHORUS
Look, Mother Earth and Radiant Sun,
look at this deadly woman,
before she can raise her hand
to spill the blood of her children,

descendants of your golden line.
I dread to think of immortal blood
shed by mortal hands!
Hold her back, Zeus-born Light! Make her stop!
Get this miserable, murderous Fury
out of the house!   1260

All for nothing, your labor in childbirth,
all for nothing, your dearly loved children,
you who passed through the perilous border
of the dark-faced Clashing Rocks.
Why has relentless anger
settled in your heart,
why this rage for death upon death?
The stain of kindred blood weighs heavy.
The gods send the killers evil pains
to echo evil crimes.   1270

FIRST BOY (*in the house*)
  No! No!   1270a

CHORUS
  Do you hear? Do you hear that child's cry?
  Oh that wretched, ill-starred woman!

FIRST BOY
  Help! How do I get away from our mother?

SECOND BOY
  I don't know how. There's no escape.

CHORUS
  Should I go in? I might prevent
  those boys from dying.

FIRST BOY
  Yes, by the gods, yes! Help us now!

SECOND BOY
She has us cornered with her sword.

CHORUS
Wretched woman, made of stone, made of iron!
I see you really have it in you   1280
to turn your deadly hand
against the boys you bore yourself.

I have only heard of one other woman
who raised her hand against her children:
Ino,° driven wild by Zeus's wife,
who made her wander far from home.
Poor woman, she plunged into the sea,
and dragged her children to unholy death.
Stepping over the seacliff's edge,
she died along with her two sons.
Is any dreadful thing impossible now?   1290
How much disaster has been caused
by the pain of women in marriage!

(*Enter Jason.*)

JASON
You women there beside the house,
is Medea inside, the perpetrator
of these terrible crimes? Has she escaped?
Unless she burrows deep in the earth
or else grows wings and flies through the air,
the royal family will make her pay.
After she killed such powerful people,
does she think she can escape scot-free?   1300
Still, I'm mainly worried about the children.
Those she abused can do the same to her,
but I am here now to save my boys.
More suffering for me if Creon's kinsmen
try to punish them for their mother's crime.

CHORUS
Poor man, you don't know all your troubles,
or you would not have said what you just did.

JASON
What is it? Does she want to kill me too?

CHORUS
The boys are dead. Their mother killed them.

JASON
What are you saying? Those words are death to me.   1310

CHORUS
Don't think of your children as among the living.

JASON
She killed them . . . where? In the house or outside?

CHORUS
If you open the doors, you will see how they died.

JASON
Servants, draw back these bolts at once,
open the doors, so I can see both evils:
the dead children and the woman I will punish.

(*Enter Medea in a winged chariot above the house, with her Sons' bodies.*)

MEDEA
Why do you keep banging on the doors
to get at the boys and me, their killer?
Don't exert yourself. If you have something to say,
I'm here, go ahead. But you'll never touch me.   1320
This chariot from my grandfather the Sun
protects me from an enemy's hands.

JASON

You abomination, most hateful of women
to the gods, to me, to the whole human race.
You were actually able to drive a sword
into sons you had borne; you've made me childless.
How can you live and see the light of the sun,
when you have committed this sacrilege
and ought to be dead? Now I see what I missed
when I brought you from that barbarian place   1330
into a Greek home. You are an evil being:
you betrayed your father and your native land.
The gods are crushing me for what you did
when you killed your brother at the family hearth
before you boarded the beautiful *Argo*.
That's how you started. Then you married me,
you bore me children and then you killed them
just because of some sexual grievance.
No Greek woman would ever do that.
To think I bound myself to you instead   1340
in a hateful, ruinous union
with an inhuman wife, a lioness
more savage than Etruscan Scylla.°
All the angry words I could hurl at you
carry no sting, you are so brazen.
To hell with you, you filthy child-killer!
All that is left for me is to mourn my fate;
I have lost the joy of my new marriage;
the children that I fathered and brought up
are gone. I'll never speak with them again.   1350

MEDEA

I could refute your speech at length,
but Father Zeus already knows
how you were treated by me and what you did.
There is no way you could reject my bed
and lead a happy life laughing at me,
you or the princess, no way that Creon

who arranged all this could throw me out
and not pay the price. So call me a lion,
or Scylla lurking on the Etruscan plain,
I've done what I had to: I've pierced your heart.   1360

JASON
But it hurts you too, you share in this pain.

MEDEA
The pain is worth it if it kills your laughter.

JASON
O children, what a vicious mother you had!

MEDEA
O boys, your father's disease destroyed you!

JASON
It was not my hand that slaughtered them.

MEDEA
No, your arrogance and your brand-new marriage.

JASON
You really think sex was a reason to kill them?

MEDEA
You think being spurned is trivial for a woman?

JASON
Yes, if she's sensible. You resent everything.

MEDEA
Well, they are gone, and that will bite deep.   1370

JASON
Oh, but they will take revenge on you.

MEDEA

The gods know which of us started this trouble.

JASON

Yes, they know your mind and it disgusts them.

MEDEA

Hate all you want. I loathe the sound of your voice.

JASON

And I loathe yours. We won't find it hard to part.

MEDEA

Then what's to be done? I too am eager for that.

JASON

Let me bury these bodies and weep for them.

MEDEA

Absolutely not. I will bury them myself
in the shrine of Hera of the Rocky Heights,
where none of my enemies can get at them   1380
or wreck their graves. Here in the land of Sisyphus
I will institute a procession and sacred rites
as atonement for this unholy murder.
Then I'll be off to the city of Erechtheus
to live with Aegeus, Pandion's son.
You will have a fitting death for a coward,
hit on the head by a piece of the *Argo*—
the bitter result of marrying me.

JASON

Let a Fury rise up to avenge these boys,
and Justice that punishes bloodshed.   1390

MEDEA

What god or spirit listens to you?
You broke your oaths, you betrayed a friend!

JASON

Ha! Abomination! Child-killer!

MEDEA

Just go home and bury your wife.

JASON

I am going, and without my children.

MEDEA

This grief is nothing. Wait till you're old.

JASON

O children, much loved!

MEDEA

By their mother, not you.

JASON

You, who killed them?

MEDEA

To punish you.

JASON

All I want is to hold them tight,
to press their sweet faces to mine.   1400

MEDEA

Now you talk to them, now you kiss them.
Before you shoved them aside.

JASON

By the gods,
just let me touch their tender skin.

MEDEA

Not possible. Your words are useless.

JASON

    Zeus, do you hear? I am shut out,
    dismissed by this vicious animal,
    this lioness stained with children's blood.
    With all my being I grieve for them
    and summon the gods to witness
    how you destroyed my children,   1410
    and will not let me touch their bodies
    or bury them in proper tombs.
    I wish I had never fathered them
    to see them slaughtered by you.

(*Exit Medea in the chariot.*)

CHORUS

    In all that Olympian Zeus watches over,
    much is accomplished that we don't foresee.
    What we expect does not come about;
    the gods clear a path for the unexpected.
    That is how things happened here.°

Notes

42 . . . *to kill the king and his daughter's new bridegroom*: Words in brackets here and throughout are considered by most scholars to be later additions to the text, sometimes inserted by actors, sometimes by scholars and editors.

134–35 *I'm sure I could hear through the double doors*: In the Greek text, the lines of lyric passages are divided differently by different editors. Groups of words conventionally numbered as separate lines may be combined in a single line, as happens here and elsewhere in the edition used for this translation.

150 *in that girl's sad song?*: In the original Greek, the Chorus refers to Medea with the word for a bride or new wife, accentuating her unsettled situation.

160 *Mighty Themis! Holy Artemis!*: Artemis: virgin goddess associated with women's transition to marriage. Themis: venerable goddess associated with justice and proper order.

233 *to buy a husband*: A bride's family paid a dowry to the groom upon her marriage.

395 *By Hecate*: Goddess associated with magic and witchcraft.

405 *Do not be mocked by this Sisyphean wedding*: In the spirit of Sisyphus, a legendary Corinthian trickster, eventually punished in Hades with the eternal task of pushing a rock uphill only to have it roll down again.

527 *but I say that it was Aphrodite*: Goddess of love; her son Eros made people fall in love by shooting them with his arrows.

543 *or a gift for singing better than Orpheus*: Legendary singer who could set animals, trees, and stones in motion; one of the Argonauts.

679 *Not to untie the foot of the wineskin . . .* : Leather container for wine in the shape of an animal, with a "foot" that served as an opening.

824 *The sons of Erectheus*: Legendary early king of Athens.

836 *in the streams of clear Cephisus*: River running through Athens.

1079 *but anger overwhelms my second thoughts*: The proper translation of this line is a matter of debate, since the same Greek word is used for "second thoughts" as for the plans they would rule out. An alternative way of interpreting the line is "Anger is the force that drives my plans."

1172 *that she was possessed by some god like Pan*: Half-man, half-goat, a pastoral god associated with wild, ecstatic behavior.

1284–85 *who raised her hand against her children: Ino*: Wife of Athamas, king of Boeotia. To strengthen the parallel with Medea, Euripides is reworking the usual version of the myth, in which Zeus's wife Hera drives Athamas mad, he kills one of their children, and Ino falls off a cliff while fleeing with the other.

1343 *more savage than Etruscan Scylla*: A sea monster with six snake heads, positioned opposite the whirlpool Charybdis, who snatched sailors out of their ships.

1419 *That is how things happened here*: The Chorus's final lines appear in almost the same form in four other plays of Euripides, which has led some scholars to conclude they are spurious.